The *Naughty*
PANCAKE

Once upon a time..

...an old woman made a pancake.

The pancake rolled across the floor.

FLOUR

See page 25.

3

It rolled past a little girl on a bike.

Next the pancake rolled past a cow.

Draw and colour.

5

Next the pancake rolled past three goats.

Next the pancake rolled past three bears.

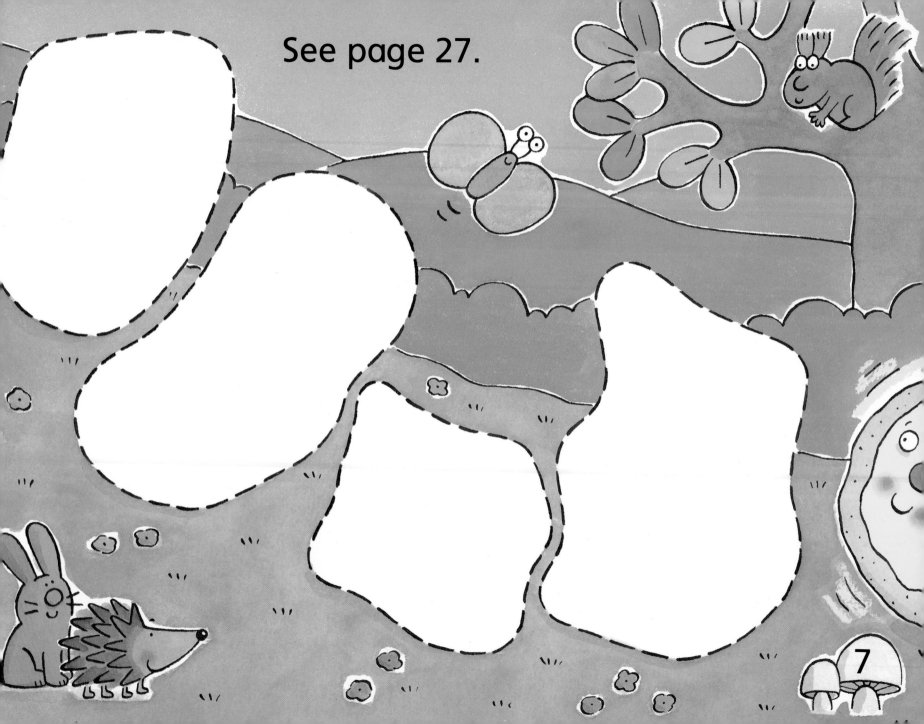

See page 27.

7

The pancake stopped. It saw a fox.

The fox started to swim across the river.

8

Draw.

9

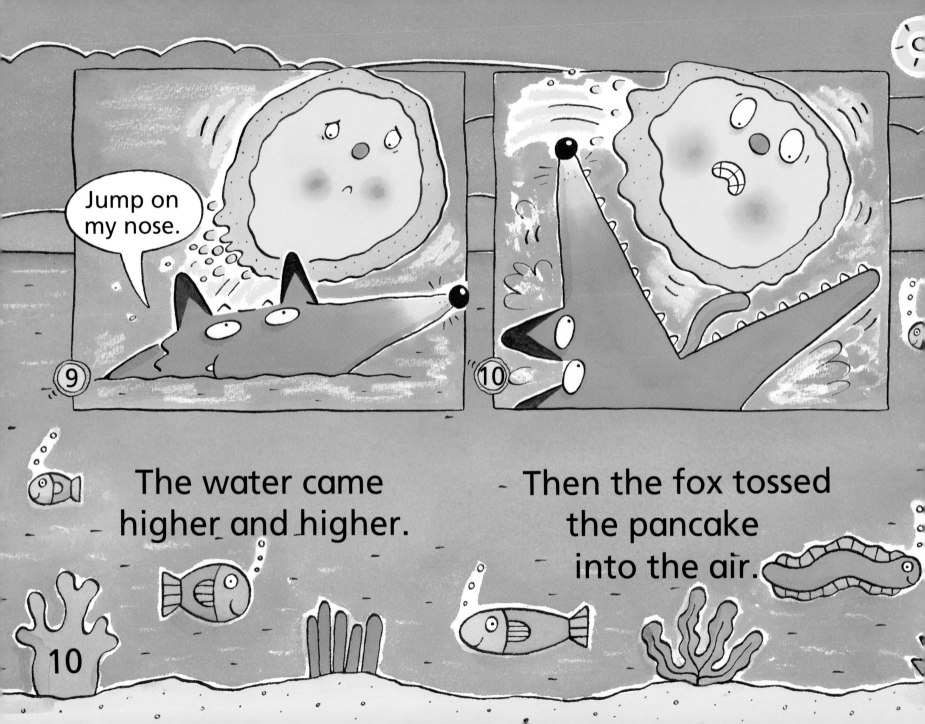

The water came
higher and higher.

Then the fox tossed
the pancake
into the air.

Roll and count.

11

That was the end
of the naughty pancake.

Stick an envelope here.

Keep your spinner inside.

13

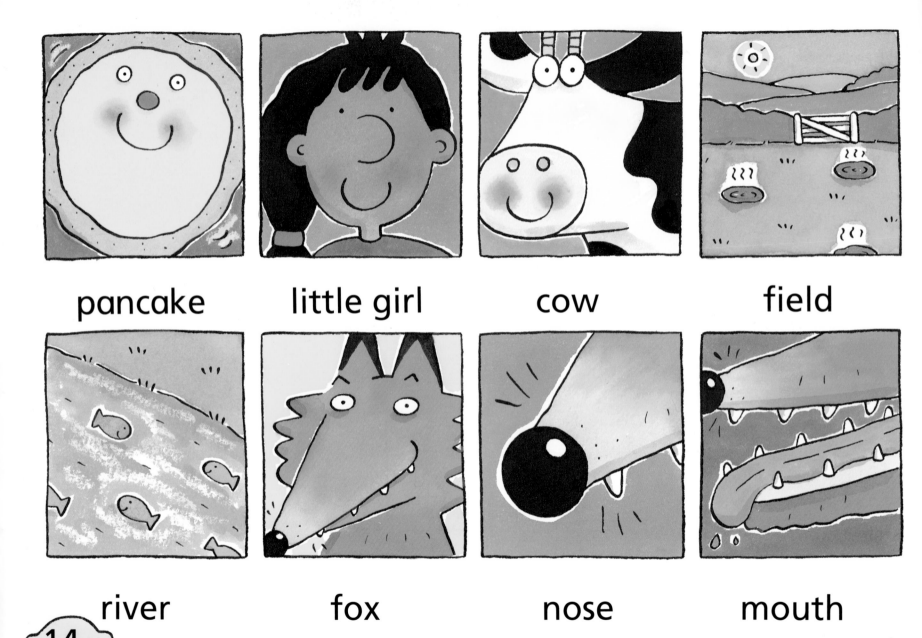

pancake   little girl   cow   field

river   fox   nose   mouth

Draw.

Hey, Diddle, Diddle

Hey, diddle, diddle

The cat and the fiddle

The cow jumped over the moon

18

Draw.

The little dog laughed
to see such fun

20

And the dish ran away
with the spoon

FIDO

See page 31.

21

cat

fiddle

cow

moon

dog

over

dish

spoon

22

Draw and join. 23

Draw.

24

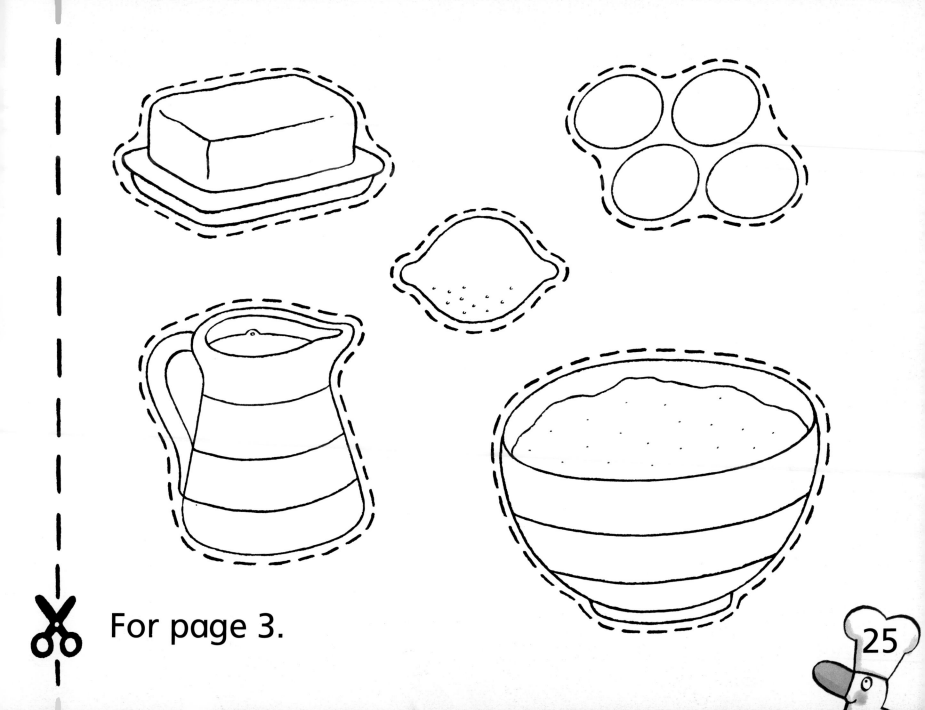

For page 3.

25

For page 7.

27

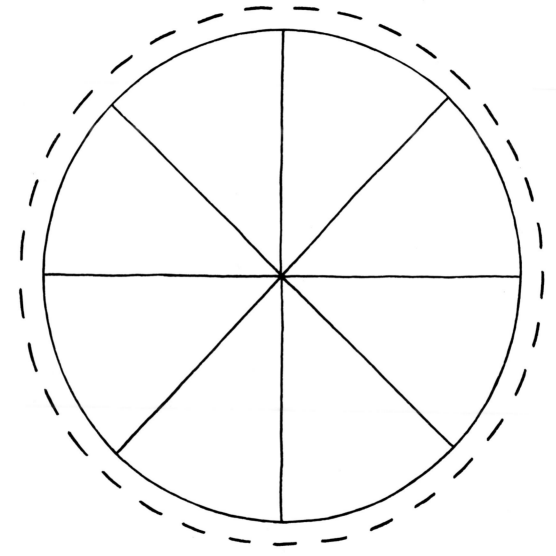

 For page 13.

For page 21.

31

For page 45.

33

For page 49.

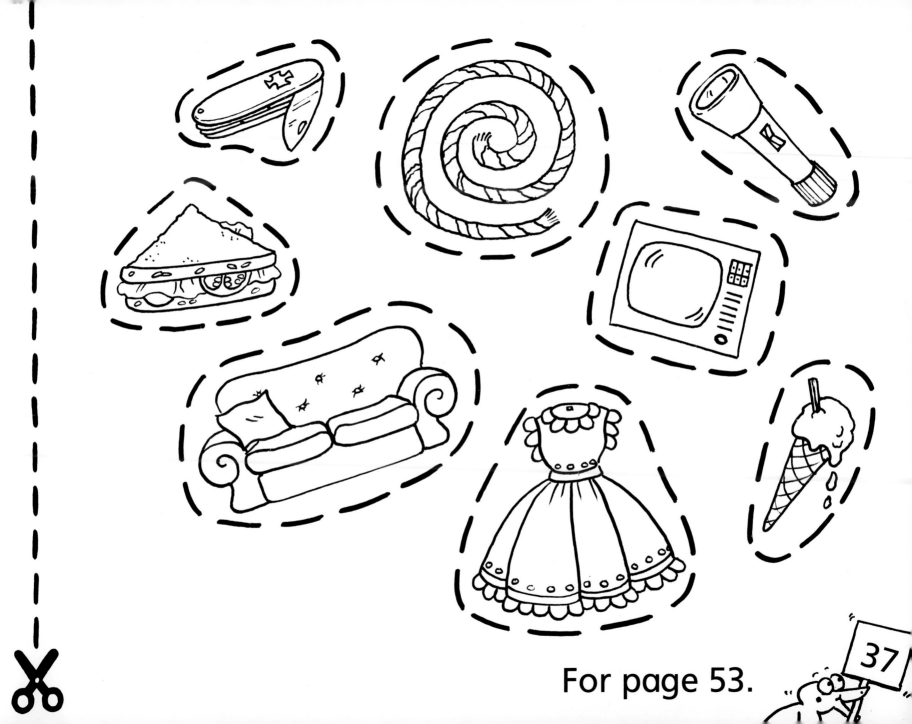

For page 53.

37

For page 59.

39

THE **BEAR** HUNT

We're all going
on a bear hunt.

We have to
run through it.

42

Draw the best route home.

43

Deep mud!

We have to walk through it.

A wide river!

We have to swim across it.

44

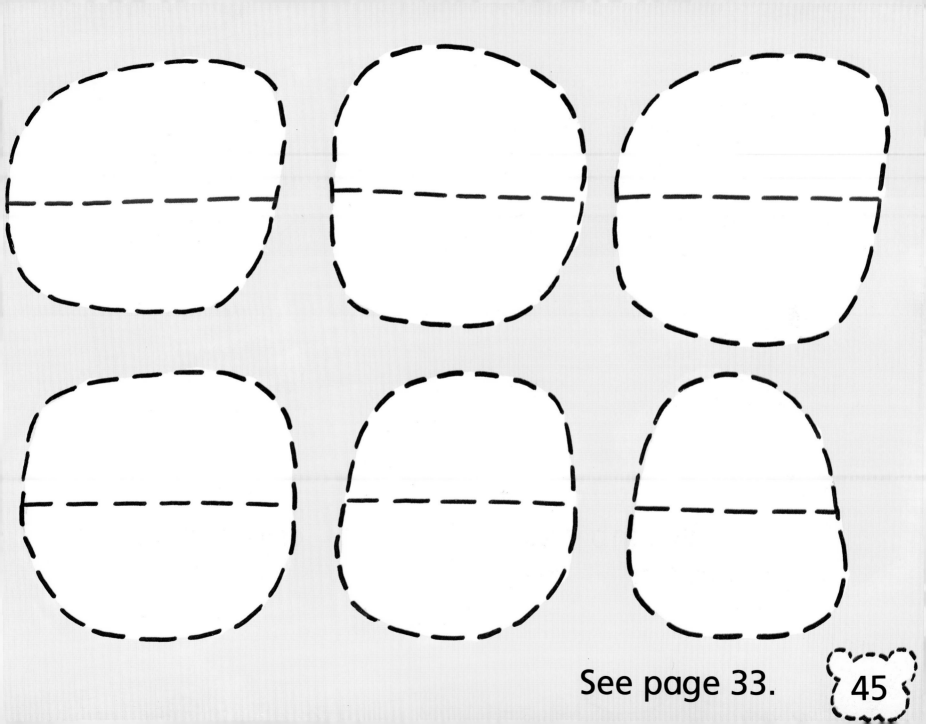

See page 33.

We have to climb over it.

We have to creep through it.

A dark cave!

We have to tiptoe inside it.

A big nose. Two big eyes.

48

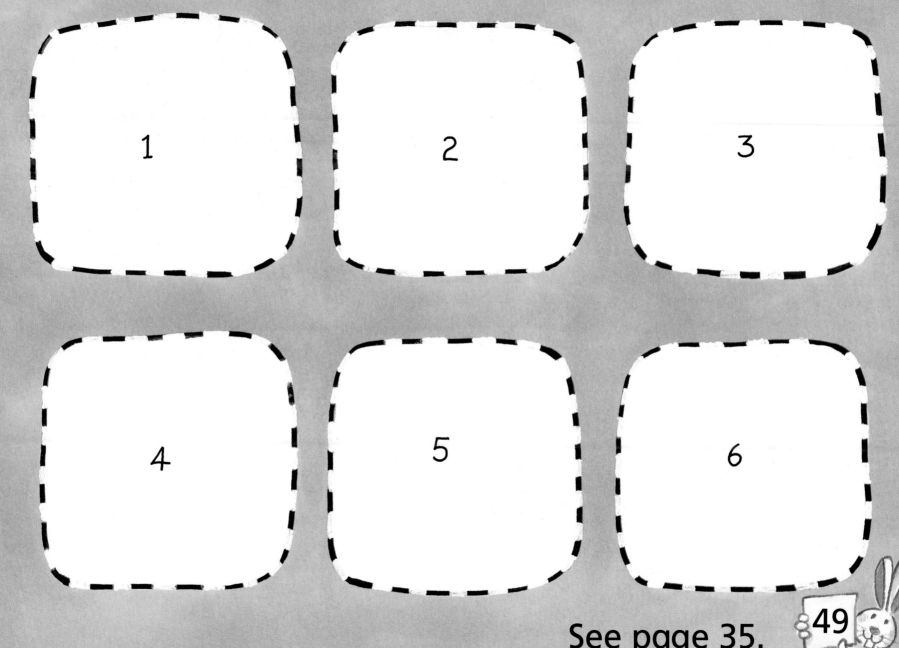

1

2

3

4

5

6

See page 35.

A big mouth.

Long claws.

Listen and point.

Help!

Help! It's a bear.

52

See page 37.

bear   long grass   deep mud   wide river

high mountain   dark forest   dark cave   run

Draw and colour.

55

56   Draw.

Mary, Mary Quite Contrary

Mary, Mary
quite contrary

How does your
garden grow?

See page 39.

With silver bells
and tiny shells

And pretty maids
all in a row

3

4

Match.

61

Mary

garden

silver bells

tiny shells

tree

pond

potato

water

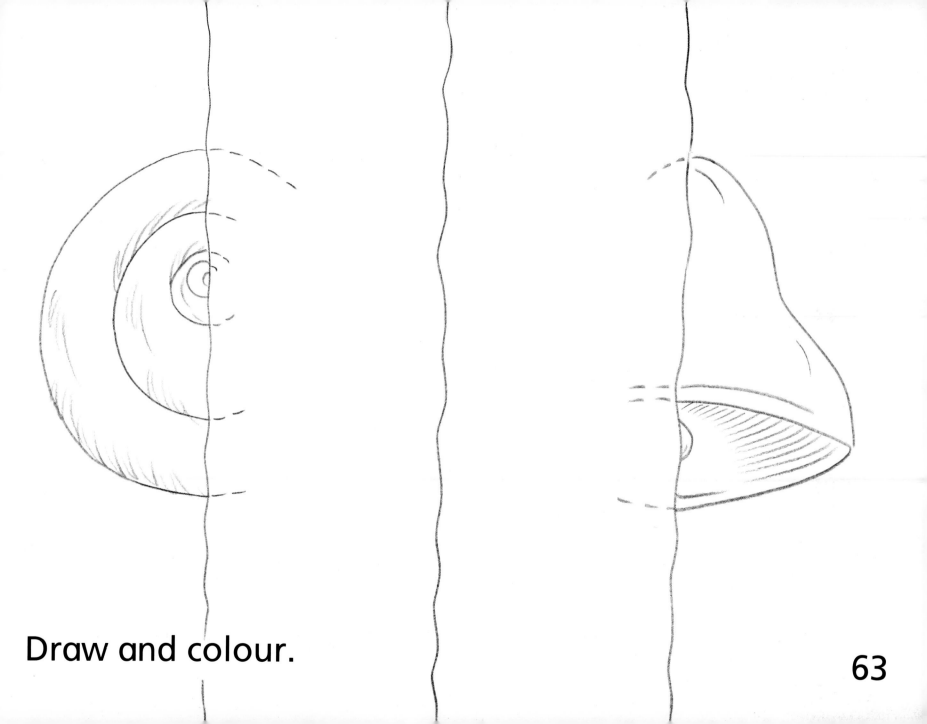

Draw and colour.

Macmillan Education
Between Towns Road, Oxford OX4 3PP, UK
A division of Macmillan Publishers Limited
Companies and representatives throughout the world

Heinemann is a registered trademark of Reed Educational & Professional Publishing Limited

ISBN 0 435 29153X

First published 1995

STORY WORLD 4 consists of:	
Pupil's Book 4	ISBN 0 435 29153X
Big Book (3 and 4)	ISBN 0 435 291599
Cassette (3 and 4)	ISBN 0 435 291572
Teacher's Book (3 and 4)	ISBN 0 435 291556

Designed by Martin Adams.

Illustrated by Sue Cony, Tania Hurt-Newton, Jacqueline East and Caroline Jayne Church.
Cover illustration by Anni Axworthy.

Printed in Thailand

2005 2004 2003 2002 2001
12 11 10 9 8 7 6 5 4

The publishers and authors would like to thank teachers
and children at the following schools and organisations
for their invaluable help in piloting this course:

Bewerley Escola d'Idiomes, Reus, Spain
Centro Educativo "Zola", Villanueva de la Cañada, Spain
Colegio Brains, Madrid, Spain
Colegio de las Irlandesas, Seville, Spain
Colegio los Rosas, Seville, Spain
Ecole Guy de Maupassant, Tours, France
Ecole Marie Curie, Villepreux, France
Scuola Elementare "E. Toti", Mestre, Italy
Hamamatsu Eigo Kenkyu Kai, Japan
Little Prince School, Tokyo, Japan
St David's School, Berro, Uruguay
Vienna International School, Austria